Mark Jarman

Signs & Wonders

JOHNS HOPKINS: POETRY AND FICTION
John T. Irwin, General Editor

Signs & Wonders

Poems by Charles Martin

The Johns Hopkins University Press
Baltimore

For Mark, Friend, colleague & admired poet —
Sewanee 2011
Charles

This book has been brought to publication with the generous assistance of the G. Harry Pouder Fund.

The Johns Hopkins University Press
2715 North Charles Street
Baltimore, Maryland 21218-4363
www.press.jhu.edu

Library of Congress Cataloging-in-Publication Data

Martin, Charles, 1942–
   Signs & wonders : poems / by Charles Martin.
      p. cm. — (Johns Hopkins: poetry and fiction)
   ISBN-13: 978-0-8018-9974-4 (hardcover : alk. paper)
   ISBN-10: 0-8018-9974-5 (hardcover : alk. paper)
   I. Title. II. Title: Signs and wonders.
   PS3563.A72327S54 2011
   811'.54—dc22   2010042463

A catalog record for this book is available from the British Library.

Special discounts are available for bulk purchases of this book. For more information, please contact Special Sales at 410-516-6936 or specialsales@press.jhu.edu.

To Johanna

Contents

Signs & Wonders

Directions for Assembly

Signs is a noun (as in DO NOT DISTURB);
Wonders (as in "with furrowed brows"), a verb.

I/ The Life in Letters

The Flower Thief

At last he struck on our block and snatched
Geraniums out of the flowerpots
And window boxes we had left unwatched,
Plucked the plants whole, took flower, stem and roots,

Danced down the street in glee and merriment,
Every so often letting out a whoop,
Asperging us with soil mix as he went,
Until he settled on an empty stoop.

And there gazed on his prizes, fascinated
By something in them only he could see,
While those who called the local precinct waited,
Watching him with or without sympathy.

He learned the essence of geranium.

We learned that the police don't always come.

Souvenir

1/
Somehow it had escaped
By the time that we had flown
Back to New York City
And on to our new home---
That slender insect, shaped
From a green husk of corn
Twisted until crickety
On a cobbled street in Rome.

2/
A Chinese emigrant,
Perched by a cardboard box,
Fashioned these vegetal
Crickets and grasshoppers;
His wiry fingers bent
And tied the sheathes to flex
In forms that would appeal
To bargain-hunting shoppers.

3/
Bagged up in plastic, tied
With little wire collars,
Like goldfish in their bowls
Waiting for adoption,
Each silent cricket vied
For euros or for dollars

And waited to be sold:
It had no other option.

4/
If it *had* been poverty,
The dull incessant grind
Of want which went unheeded,
That snatched up and replanted
Him here in Italy,
What put it in his mind
To sell what no one needed
And almost no one wanted?

5/
Was it just ignorance
Of the foreign market---
That and the optimist's
More than half-filled glass?
"What every Roman wants
Is a good cornhusk cricket---
With a few deft ties and twists
My dream will come to pass!"

6/
That isn't even funny:
He sleeps on a low cot in
A single crowded room
On the shift assigned him.
He owes his landlord money.
He fears he's been forgotten

By his family back home:
Will Good Luck ever find him?

7/
Perhaps: *Que sera, sera.*
But now among the fakes,
The *faux* Gucci scarves and shoes,
The double-A batteries
And plastic ephemera,
He stands by his box and makes
A life he did not choose,
From what would otherwise

8/
Be overlooked as waste
(As he himself might be
In this world's new order):
But how shall the genuine
Not be wholly effaced
From life and memory
And taught to slip the border---
How, if not by design?

Some Kind of Happiness

A windblown grain of happiness
Has just now taken residence
Between the moistened surfaces
Of eye and lid: I blink and wince,
Not recognizing it as such,
And then I grimace to expel
What I can feel but cannot touch,
This moonlet torn from Planet Hell,
Whose photo, magnified, would show
A wilderness of jagged peaks
And icy crevices below.
It threatens to stay on for weeks,
And with no fixed plan traverses
The jellied pond that runs with tears,
Paying no mind to my curses.
Then suddenly it disappears.

What kind of happiness was this?

One more likely than another:
Briefly here, abruptly gone---bliss,
If not unalloyed with bother.

The Sacred Monsters

The legend, built up over many years,
That told of how the spells the monsters cast
Reduced the hapless children to hot tears
And left the grown-ups they became aghast
And swaddled in unmanageable fears
Originating in the nightmare past---
That legend needs revising, it appears,
Now that we see the monsters plain at last:

How this one, backed into a corner, snarls,
While that one rears to strike, but must give way
Before these oldsters from the suburbs, clad
In polyester leisurewear, who say
How pleased they are to be here.
                            Then, "Mom, Dad,
I'd like you both to meet my good friend Charles…"

Words to Utter at Nightfall

So here I am in Oakwood, a funeral
park built in 19th-century Syracuse,
   tracing out names while windblown snow swirls
     down at my ankles. December, twilight:

another failed quest for immortality
come to completion under a polished grey
   stone---but tonight I halt before it,
     stopped by its one-word inscription: UTTER

*

"*Utter?*" Say what, I ask myself cluelessly:
If UTTER *had* been somebody's cognomen,
   who would have raised this stone, neglecting
     either a given name or initials?

And UTTER lacks apparent connection to
any of many words it may come before:
   "bliss," say, or "rot"---intensifying
     joy in the outcome, or indignation

at learning that oblivion isn't a
concept, merely. When once we eliminate
   noun and adjective, only verb is
     left to consider. So I consider

UTTER a sharply worded imperative,
bitten in stone, unknown as to origin,
   aimed, it may be, at finding someone
      who goes off rambling in cemeteries,

hoping to be instructed by randomness,
hoping, among the dead ends so evenly
   spaced out in ordered rows, to find the
      one that might signify: *Here continue*

*

Easy to say, but where is continuance?
For certain, unaccompanied UTTER is
   awkward at best---an unvoiced, barked-out
      syllable trailed by a *schwa*, dissolving

in the thin night air, cold and companionless,
unheard by anyone, unresponded to.
   Take it, then: weave it into measure's
      ancient invention, this shopworn form, now

frayed at the edges, far from original:
use it to make an evensong utterance,
   passed on by one whose heartfelt wish is
      not to have either the first or last word

Mind in the Trees

But Wallace, what if there were, say,
Three hundred of them in one tree?
Of how many minds would you be?
I saw three hundred here one day---
Not blackbirds, since not every black
Bird's a *black*bird---these were crows,
So densely driven, you'd suppose
The branches of the tree would crack.
Yet the tree didn't seem weary
Of bearing them without a fuss---
One of the few eponymous
Oaks of Oakwood Cemetery.
The next day came three hundred more
And formed a second colony
On branches of another tree;
They spread across its upper floor.
Day after, a prodigious din
Proclaimed the transfer was complete:
All the tall trees across the street
Appeared to have been settled in.
This was in autumn. They had flown
From the bare cornfields west of us
To spend their nights in Syracuse.

At first light they would be long gone.
I'd have to have a mind of crow
To tell you where it was they went,
Although I think that their intent
Was plain enough for us to know:
To feed as well as they were able
On gleanings from some barren field,
Or test what a town dump would yield
In scraps scraped from a kitchen table.
From where they'd been, they'd all fly back
To our neighborhood and roost
Right around dusk: a sable host,
A giant beating wing of black,
Dissolving until each crow finds
Its nightly perch.
                    Regarding their a-
bidance in our area,
I was myself of several minds:
Their raucousness by night and morning,
The paintballs of their excrement
(Mixed, it would seem with fresh cement)
That dropped among us without warning,
Clearly would not gain them favor.
What would, then? Their ability
To make do on the little we
Allow them, and, indeed to carve a
Niche, however scant and dire
From our gleanings and our rot
Speaks well of them, though we may not.
It's also easy to admire
The way they seem to get along,

The nice civility each shows
(Or seems to show) his fellow crows,
Despite the discords of their song.
And there's the beauty of their flight
Whether they glide, now high, now low,
Or struggle though grey squalls of snow,
Racing against impending night;
Or when they form a canopy,
A treetop-level aggregate---
Each one a fine black cuneate
Shape on the lemon yellow sky;
It seemed each little mark they made
Was capable, collectively,
Of making one text of each tree,
A book whose upturned page displayed
The tree's own thought.
                              And then, one day,
The first or second day of spring,
At sunrise, all of them took wing
At once and hoarsely flew away,
Not to return until next fall
With a noise like blackboard-grating chalk.
I'm practicing a crow-like squawk
To greet them when I hear their call.

Autopsychography

Fernando Pessoa, *Autopsycographia*

The poet knows just how to feign.
So very thorough his pretense is,
That he pretends to have the pain
He honestly experiences.

Those who read the poet's verses
As they read them, keenly feel
Not the *two* pains he confesses,
But just their own, which is unreal.

So round and round in every season,
Upon its tracks this gaily smart
Toy train goes on, beguiling reason,
And it is called the human heart.

Support

Support is what the film of oily dust
Is put upon and slowly bonded to
Until it forms a thin, ambivalent crust
That disappears when there comes into view

Whatever we are here today to see:
A vase of flowers, Wolfe dying at Quebec,
A virgin with an infant on her knee,
Some woman grinning at Toulouse-Lautrec.

If it cannot be said to face the wall,
There's nonetheless a wall or ledge or shelf
Supporting it, though the provisional-
ity of *that* support says that support itself

Moves through such portals, all of which depend
On yet another and so never end.

East Side, West Side

1/ Vermeer at the Frick: His *Mistress and Maid*

Light flickers gaily over those surfaces
that, in this painting, represent what, if not
    beauty and pleasure, health and value?
       Framed by the background, the homely servant,

whose downcast glance suggests her uneasiness,
presents a note appearing to startle her
    seated mistress, who must have found it
       either unwelcome or unexpected

if not unwelcome. We cannot ever know
if what she had begun writing one lover
    was interfered with by another's
       well-timed or untimely importuning.

Soon, other readings, each just as possible,
will come to press their claims on the spectator.
    But we can say no more for certain
       than that there *has* been an interruption;

unconscious act and conscious reflection were
caught as she touched her chin with the fingertips
    of her left hand, while from her right, she
       let the pen drop to the covered table.

So, if I claim Vermeer must have wanted this
uneasy painting read as a secular
    Annunciation, where the one picked
        happens to be neither maid nor maiden,

I mean it just as a thought experiment:
there's not the slightest hint of submissiveness
    in her demeanor, and the drama
        played out about her is her own doing.

Nor do I find it even implausible
to see the maid as angelic messenger:
    in an Annunciation, brightness
        flows into darkness, and so transforms it,

while here, a girl constrained by her poverty
briefly enters a plane of great privilege;
    whatever right she has to be here
        is one that she has been granted merely.

But this is not about the inequality
inherent in a common relationship,
    nor will some god reduce the mistress
        to the sealed chamber of his abidance:

This is about the free play of consciousness
in steady light that limns and illuminates
    those whom it falls upon: the favored
        few, constrained only by what they've chosen.

She'll leave this afternoon or this evening;
she'll change out of that sable-lined satin robe,
  put on something a bit more modish
    and less conspicuous, flag a taxi,

and after zipping down on Fifth Avenue,
she'll meet a friend for drinks at the Century
  Club and then leave to catch a red-eye
    flight to the Netherlands on KLM.

2/ John Koch at the New-York Historical Society:
   The Party

Early evening: the summer party people
meet in a large, airy, sparsely furnished room,
sorting themselves into duets and trios
       for conversation.

All except one, who leans out from a window:
why, that one's André, the long-lost friend whom I
last saw years ago! Odd, to recognize him
       just from his posture,

even before I turn to check the legend,
Key to The Party*: Number* 8, *A. Kimbrell,*
pianist. A student of Koch's wife, Dora,
       (Number 3, speaking

to another pianist and a model,
Numbers 5 and 4.) With no one to talk to,
self-reliant André ensconces himself
       in his own niche, while

out of sight behind him, the conversations
open, as old friends introduce *their* friends to
recent strangers met in the elevator
       on their way up here;

who, as the *Key* tells us, are painters, critics,
dealers, models, pianists, wives and close friends:
nobody famous but our host and *his* friend,
      Raphael Soyer.

All now find themselves in a complex fiction,
posed, disposed as couples adjoining threesomes
linked to other couples by tightly rhyming
      postures and gestures;

groups are dissolved and then reconstituted
as the eye responds to the overlapping
figures arranged according to the subtle
      rule of perspective.

Yet it's elegiac, this summer party,
for, though the (mostly) young are clearly taken
with one another and their situation,
      none has yet noticed

how very cool the colors of the room are
in the fading light, and how the wind that's just
stirred the lacy curtains has somehow also
      lengthened the shadows.

All too soon, that moment of watches glanced at,
looks exchanged; of thanking the host and hostess,
as with a show of genuine reluctance
      guests make their exit.

I can picture André, now turning back to
find the party over, the room left vacant---
ashtrays full, glasses empty. Another day
    of wine and poses.

Facing outward, perhaps he had a glimpse of
what lay ahead: law school, books read and written,
works and days of environmental---not a
    piano's---action.

To Himself

Though they seem always much to be desired,
The lives we cannot live are far more wearing
Than the one we do. If we feel ourselves mired
In its contingencies, committed to sharing
Our tatty picnic blanket with the uncaring,
Or wasting treasure in defense of relations
Forever in need of, or beyond, repairing;
If we've grown bored with manning the feckless
    stations,
It's only that those other lives, our creations,
Weightless themselves, oppress us until we falter;
So, weakened by their effortless evasions,
We learn *this* late that the only way to alter
That situation is to leave off pursuing,
And try to begin to do what we are doing.

Brooklyn in the Seventies

1/

In all the years that I lived there, I doubt
I once imagined there would come a time
When I would learn that I had been priced out
Of Brooklyn's 19th-century sublime.
Back then it seemed much likelier to me
That I would see my small investment go
Belly-up, taken by the undertow
Of our increasing urban anomy
Until the shrinking figures shrank to naught:
A zero for the brownstone that I'd bought.

2/

Yet I persisted: property comes with
The fictions by which it's inhabited.
I lived in not a brownstone but a myth
About a brownstone, as I often said.
Brooklyn was where I'd wanted to debut,
The cozy safe but always edgy home
I didn't quite succeed in coming from,
Although the Brooklynites I later knew
Shared memories that helped me to restore
A childhood that I hadn't had before.

3/

For Brooklyn is, or was then, all about
The joys of restoration and repair:

A brownstone, once the fortified redoubt
Of feuding gangsters or the unkempt lair
Of junkies, went from shooting gallery
To showcase in---let's say eight years or ten
Of tearing down and building up again,
With never any kind of guarantee
That spouse or partner would be standing by
There at the end, if just to say good-bye.

4/

The other outcome happened quite a lot
In those days. Many couples would discover
That one was satisfied, the other not.
The one who wasn't would take on a lover,
Or take off suddenly for parts unknown,
Leaving the one who was self-satisfied
And putting one's now-outgrown self aside,
For self-discovery meant moving on
To find what would suffice and might fulfill:
One couldn't find oneself by keeping still.

5/

I knew two Sisters who had left their order,
And when I asked what made them both decide
To venture out into a world much weirder,
"It was the stillness, mainly," one replied,
"People began to ask us what we thought
Of clergy getting married and The Pill.
We hadn't thought much of such things, until
They started asking us."

                         "Soon we were out

And living here in Brooklyn, where you find us,"
The other said, "Where other vows now bind us."

6/
Yes, selves were in a frenzy of commotion,
And those beyond their expiration dates
Were being tossed despite years of devotion.
So, whether by one's doing or by fate's,
One found oneself in an unlikely place
(And back then Brooklyn more than filled the bill
For sheer unlikeliness) in Clinton Hill
Or Bedford Stuyvesant, and with a face
One hadn't chosen, one was soon immersed
In a role which one hadn't yet rehearsed.

7/
The role may have been unimportant: all
That mattered was it couldn't be defended
By older people: was what one might call
Unscripted, improvised: and always ended
At a goal which, once reached, would no more seem
To be the end one had so long intended:
"The coach stopped, the door opened, he descended."
Beyond such twaddle lay another theme,
Rich with the still-unriddled mysteries
Of life in Brooklyn in the Seventies.

This Organizing Solitude

> I have thought that my paintings of gorillas
> in some sense constituted an autobiography.
> —Miquel Barcelo

1/

Your *Life in Letters* asks a rearrangement
Of that very thing---better look before you
        Leap: this can't be done in stages,
It's yes or no, commitment or estrangement.
I mean if, say, a year from now you're bored, who
        Would even know where your cage is?
No one, is who. And only feats of patience
Will allow you access to those illuminations

2/

For which you've left life, family and *Heimat*.
Sometimes a strange new character emerges
        When you've disposed of all the clutter:
"Hello, it's me! Yes, *me*! Where *am* I? I'm at
        No. ——, Rue Morgue." The poor concierge is
        Heard by M. Dupin to mutter,
"What an ape..." It's true that your decision
May lead to changes that none of us can envision;

3/

Although each metamorphosis leaves traces
Of the old order, once across the sill, a
        Transformation of your past is

Bound to kick in. This usually effaces
Whatever in you isn't a gorilla
    Dreaming of your mountain fastness.
The only issue after that is whether
The forefinger and thumb will learn to work together.

Theory Victorious

You'll know for certain that it's happened when you
See how the famished diner spurns his dinner
Only to fall with relish on the menu---
Then you'll know Theory's been declared the winner.

II/ Some Romans

On a Roman Perfume Bottle

The Romans were not meek,
And often the results
Of their inventive labors,
Towers and catapults,
Went rumbling off to wreak
Havoc on their neighbors;

This tiny, cooled-down state
Of a once-ardent passion
Knows nothing of those wars;
But served, in its own fashion,
The imperious dictate
Of Venus's with Mars.

Ara Pacis

The white procession halts at the Altar of Peace
To give thanks for war ended on such splendid terms,
And someone deposits a shitstained lump of fleece
On the high marble table where it writhes and squirms,
Unquietly bleating, legs slipping and flailing,
And any prayer of its will be unavailing.

Ovid to His Book

(Tristia, I/1)

Off with you now, my little book, and go
to the city I am barred from, to my woe---
from Outer Nowhere all the way to Rome.
---Of course, I'm envious that I can't come
myself, and had to send *you*---poorly wrought,
lacking revision's second, better, thought
and all refinement---on this hopeless mission
to show an exile's poems and condition.

A *purple* jacket? Be sensible, my book,
go for a serious, more somber look:
forget your title page's ornamented
letters or hand-made paper, cedar-scented
with deckled edges, trimmed in costly gold
to keep away destructive dust and mold:
you needn't fear remaindering---nor is
longevity the greatest of your worries.

Books are well made when fortune's favor pours
down on their authors---as it won't on yours.
Since it's *my* fortune you should keep in mind,
display no polish of whatever kind:
better that you seem rugged and unkempt,
a ragamuffin with complete contempt

for random stains and blots: each will appear,
to those who notice it, an author's tear.

Go on your way now, book, and speak for me
in places that I love, but cannot be,
saluting those whom I have come to meet
on metrical, if on no other, feet.
To those who ask of you, "How *is* our Ovid?"
say that although I haven't yet recovered
my health and happiness, I'm pleased to give
thanks to the god by whose gift I still live.

Say what you need to and then say no more:
say nothing of what I'm being punished for---
how long do you imagine I'd survive
if I were to lead off *The News at Five*?
When biting words offend you, just recall
the best defense is often none at all,
and if you'd really have my exile end,
go find us both an influential friend,

someone who sighs to think of my removal,
and when he reads *you* gives his tears' approval,
silently praying Caesar will relent
his anger and reduce my punishment---
we trust the gods won't make that one atone,
for seeking to ease *my* loss, with his own,
and that the Prince will soon be quieted
so I may die at home in my own bed!

But when you have complied with my directive,
You'll still find some who'll say that you're defective.
If critics must consider the circumstance
and time of any act, you have a chance:
one needs, in order to compose in measure,
a mind at rest in solitude and leisure,
not one that's clouded over with its fear
because the executioner draws near!

A judge who understands this will applaud,
and reading, pardon---though the work be flawed:
put Homer in a pickle great as mine
and watch *his* genius suddenly decline!
So have no care for the best-seller list,
and give no thought to readers who resist
your many charms: my fortunes must be raised
before anything *I* write will be praised!

When I was fortunate, I hungered for
stardom, celebrity, and much, much more;
it now suffices that I do not hate
the poems that have brought me to this state,
the cleverness I suffer for---and from!
So go in my place now and visit Rome
as I would do, and walk about, and look
upon its wonders---would I were my book!

Don't think, because you come here from abroad,
you'll pass among the populace ignored!
I fear my notoriety may hurt you;
if any guardian of female virtue

finds you, because of me, fit for rejection,
offer your title page for his inspection:
"That work you think I am---which I am not,
The Art of Love, deserved the thumps it got!"

Do you suppose I'll send you, book of mine,
to Caesar's home high on the Palatine?
I beg forgiveness of that lofty site---and
of its deities---but I am still frightened:
the blast that struck me issued from that hill!
Some of its gods, I know, are merciful,
but how can I not shudder with alarm
merely to think of those that did me harm?

The dove you wounded, hawk, now quakes with dread
whenever feathers rustle overhead;
delivered from the wolf's embrace, the lamb
is loath to leave the sheepfold and its dam;
the Sea of Icarus assumed the name
of that young lad who flew too near the flame:
beware, my book, observe the bottom feeders,
be satisfied with ordinary readers.

From here, I can't be sure which will prevail,
whether you should rely on oars or sail;
just let the situation be your guide:
if you come near him when he puts aside
the business of the day, and clemency,
the thought of it, supplants his rage at me;
if someone, as you shake with doubt and fear,
whispers an introduction in his ear,

approach---and on a day more fortunate
than your own master, you'll improve his state,
for if my wound's not fatal, it can be
cured only by the one who wounded me.
My fears are numerous, my hopes are scant,
so do not injure what you would advance---
don't rouse the sleeping lion in his den,
or give him cause to punish me again.

But let's not think of that, dear little tome;
rather, let's think of you, soon to be home,
back at the townhouse, in the studio
upon your shelf, and with you, in a row,
your brothers all in chronologic order,
the products of my diligence and ardor.
Most of them show their titles openly
for anyone at all who passes by:

There are, however, three that shun the light,
maneuvering to keep far out of sight,
huddled together at a safe remove:
they teach---who doesn't know?---the art of love.
I recommend you stay away from those,
that, like Telegonus or Oedipus,
slew their own father. If you have affection
for your parent, fly from their seduction!

Beside them stand my *Metamorphoses*,
survivors of my fortune's exequies;
what I owe them, I hope you may amend:
my daily funeral here at world's end.

I bid you tell them now that my own fate
resembles one of them in his changed state,
no more as I once was---and now much less,
with sorrow in the place of happiness.

I've more to tell you, book, if you should ask,
but that would only keep you from your task,
and if I filled you up with all my trouble,
the one who carried you would be bent double;
and you, if all that *you* did was repine,
would not be recognized as one of mine!
The road is long---hurry, while I bemoan
abidance in this land far from my own.

Three Sonnets from the Romanesco of G.G. Belli

1/ The Good Soldiers

As soon as any earthly sovereign
Receives a slight in his own estimation,
"You are the enemy---" he tells his nation,
"---Of this or that king! Go and do him in!"

His people, eager to avoid the pen
Or some such pleasantry I will not mention,
Hoist muskets and ship out with the intention
Of making war on French or Englishmen.

So, for some martinet's fantastic whims,
The sheep come stumbling back into the stall
With broken skulls and mutilated limbs.

They toss their lives as children toss a ball,
As if that old whore, Death, who lops and trims
The human race, comes only when we call.

2/ The Spaniard

A Spaniard claimed that everything in Rome---
Its churches, castles, its antiquities,
Its fountains, columns, palaces---all these
Were equaled or improved upon at home.

To put him down and keep myself amused,
I one day went and bought at the bazaar
Inside the Pantheon a hefty pair
Of testicles a sheep had lately used.

I boxed them up quite nicely and I had him
Take a good look. I said: "These very ballocks
Are the same two that once belonged to Adam."

He first seemed quite astounded by my trick,
And then he said: "These *are* impressive relics,
But in *my* country, we've got Adam's prick."

3/ The Coffee House Philosopher

Men are the same, on our little sphere,
As coffee beans poured in the coffee mill;
One leads, one follows, one brings up the rear,
But a single fate is waiting for them all.

Often they change their places in the parade,
The greater beans displace the weak and small,
And all press toward the exit with its blade,
Through which, ground into powder, they must spill.

The hand of fortune stirs them all together,
And that is how men live here with their fellows,
Going around in circles with each other,

Lost in the depths, or struggling in the shallows,
Not comprehending what or why or whether,
Until death lifts his little cup and swallows.

III/ Near Jeffrey's Hook

The Twentieth Century in Photographs

Different faces, formats all the same:
A profile set beside a frontal view
And nothing else included in the frame
Save, at the bottom, for a coded row

Of numbers dashes letters that replaces
A name best left unsaid by those who knew it.
Two aspects of one face there, not two faces.
Behind each is a blank wall, we intuit,

More like an edge each one could be tipped over,
Once photographed. Impossible to read
These inexpressive faces and recover
The thoughts of those who have been so long dead,

Who died, in fact, before the photographer
Had time to fix them in his clear solution.
Although their eyes meet ours now, we are
Still not there yet: no stay of execution.

Poem for the Millennium

Prophets proclaim   the perfected hour,
Extinctions everywhere   endanger survival,
Terminate the terrestrial   tenure of mankind:
Off on a tiny   atom-bombed atoll,
On our waste waters   a dragon waxes,
A saurian sprung   from seed mutated
Becomes a behemoth   that blocks out the sun,
As it lifts off on loathsome   leathery wings,
Eager to seize   and sack our cities;
The anxious await   an asteroid's impact,
While Gaia groans   at the gaping earth
And fires flicker   from faults long-hidden,
Deep as all delving;   in utter darkness
The earth's shelves   shift and shatter,
Drifting apart;   dormant volcanoes
Revive and vent   their viscous magma;
Great walls of water   wash beaches away;
A terrible toll   is taken in lives.

    Now, at the New Year   another menace:
A viral invader   evades our defenses,
And stunned computers   convulse and crash;
The bright screens before us   go blank at once,
Their voices vanish   into the void.
The match is struck: strife and disorder
Spread from the cities   out to their suburbs
Of merchandise malls   and manicured lawns

Wend their way   to the trackless woods
Where bearded boors   in faded blue jeans
And flannel shirts   feast upon freeze-dried
Provender pressed   into packets of tinfoil,
Endlessly brooding   on engines of evil
And hatching horrors   under their hats.

Some faintest flaw   sends feelers out,
A hairline fault   finds its way to the surface;
The cleft becomes   a network of crackling,
And the vase shivers,   shocked into shards:
Chaos increasing   causes such failures.
Lightly leaping   a break in the line,
With woven words   we ward it off
Over the silence: caesura that stands for
The fell fissure   we feel underfoot.

Who Knows What's Best?

I am the decider and I decide what's best.
—George W. Bush

1/

The ones we bomb to liberate
Have really got an attitude:
Despite the care we demonstrate
The ones we bomb to liberate
From tyranny respond with hate:
How's that for sheer ingratitude?
The ones we bomb to liberate
Have really got an attitude.

2/

And those we torture to set free
Have got no cause to sigh and groan:
As we export democracy
The ones we torture to set free
Are stripped of human dignity
In prisons no worse than our own.
No, those we torture to set free
Have got no cause to sigh and groan.

3/

And what is all this fuss about
Who knows what's best? The ones in charge,
Believe me, don't have any doubt.
Say what? Is all this fuss about

The liberties we trample out?
Our nation's powerful and large,
So what is all this fuss about?
Who knows what's best? The ones in charge.

Getting Carded

We couldn't know what we would lose
When the ENDANGERED SPECIES sign
Began to turn up in our zoos---
A small white card propped up on a
Shelf in front of the cage or pen
Of one selected for this honor,
Translated from its habitat
Into a compact modern flat.

By what ENDANGERED, or by whom,
It couldn't know until too late:
One day it woke up in this room
Where it patrols compulsively
The borders of its shrunken state
And stares at what it cannot see:
Far dominions, other powers.
Its glance keeps on avoiding ours.

You wonder why it didn't learn,
Although, quite frankly, it seems not
Even to share your mild concern.
Time to move on: the fourth grade class
Behind us wants to claim our spot
And press its faces to the glass.
We leave ENDANGERED and its text
And wonder who'll get carded next.

For the End of the Age of Irony

Why, if it's gone now, is there this leftover
ambience seeping into and staining the
    fabric of our conversation,
        like red wine spilled on the bone-white sofa?

Though its infrequent sightings are treated as
cases of mere mistaken identity,
    and though its age may now be ended,
        it seems that irony's not quite done for---

one old employer pays it occasional
visits on Sundays, riding a trolley car
    out to the suburbs where it lingers,
        though much diminished, as he informs us:

"Odd to contrast its formerly vigorous
habits of growth, its flourishing presence in
    those lives to which it once seemed central,
        with its now-marginal situation

off in the corner, fusty leaves withering---
if only we'd remembered to water it
    every so often, yes, if only
        with our crocodile tears, if only...."

Such insincere remorse may remind you of
how you enjoyed the late Donald Justice's

version of Baudelaire's evasive
 elegy made for the clumsy servant,

wondering only whether the French version
should be preferred for *its* insincerity
 over the translator's nostalgia
  for those emotions he never suffered.

It may seem strange that an inability
to speak of irony without irony
 argues more clearly for its value
  than any argument it's not part of,

or that nostalgia is the more keenly felt
out of proportion to the experience
 causing it, as a magnifying
  lens will make any poor micro, macro.

But you were always taken with artifice,
drawn to it like a sow to a truffle bed,
 weren't you, finding it a refuge
  from the unbearably lofty motive,

as from the unendurable punditry
of those whom mere self-interest animates;
 you saw it deftly undermining
  acres of wind-powered bloviators,

and noticed how, when we get too serious
in its defense, it vanishes utterly;

ironists surely would consider
        such an odd outcome as---well, ironic.

Better to leave its fragile and fugitive
self to recover, with our negligence
        offering all it really needs for
            any eventual restoration:

which someone someday (on one reality,
many perspectives) will lightly illustrate
        merely by letting you know that the
            beautiful necktie you're wearing, isn't.

Near Jeffrey's Hook

1/
No one is living here now who can say
What it was once called by the Lenapé,

Who must have given it a proper name
Before the Dutchmen and the British came.

They lived here lightly, nourished on demand,
And signified their tenure of the land

With firesites, with mounds of oyster shells,
Flint arrowheads, clay bowls, dog burials---

Remnants that come to light now and again.
Their present was as it had always been

While ours isn't what it used to be,
So we imagine what we cannot see:

Propulsive figures in a bark canoe
Whose blades divide the river's stream in two,

Now gliding skillfully along the shore,
An image from a present long before.

2/

We see what they could never have imagined:
One Eighty-first Street's still-evolving pageant

Of up and coming keeps on coming up,
Bright oddments caught in a kaleidoscope---

A single orange skin, expertly twirled
Will wrap itself three times around the world!

Here are peeled oranges in plastic sacks,
Electric storefronts filled with shirts and slacks

Advertised at nearly wholesale prices;
Here someone peddles sugar-syrup ices,

And in the window next door is a frieze
Of chickens spitted on rotisseries;

---And if the river where the street concludes
No longer summons up archaic moods,

On certain evenings it reflects Monet's
Sunsets of pinks and oily, buttery grays...

3/

We thought that what was possible must be,
Moved to invention by the necessity

Of finding needs that inventions satisfied:
Necessity might be a stream too wide

To get the goods across in half an hour.
As we became more certain of our power,

We couldn't help but act on what we knew:
The inconvenience of the river grew

More noticeable until everyone
Agreed that something really must be done:

A river, though it isn't real estate,
Can be exploited just like real estate.

Laid end-to-end, sticks of dynamite filled
The hollow tubes mechanically drilled

Into Manhattan's ancient upper crust,
Which cracked up in a sudden cloud of dust.

4/
The river yields, whatever its intention,
To engineering's silver-spanned suspension…

Blasting left floors and windows all askew
In buildings that went up in all the new

Neighborhoods along the northwest ridge,
A bonus from construction of the Bridge.

Five years ago we moved to one such, built
In 1925. A perceptible tilt

Was proven when we let a marble roll
From one room to another down the hall

Until it stopped to listen by the door,
Explosions having modified the floor

Three quarters of a century ago.
Further explosions brought a steady flow

Of refugees into the neighborhood,
Fleeing the tyranny of race and blood.

5/
Locked in the languages they spoke from birth,
And as unable to assert their worth

To the indifferent here as to resume
The lives they might have died escaping from,

They'd long since learned that all they had been born to
Was now replaced by nothing to return to,

Yet they were fortunate, they understood,
From what they'd learned of fortunes, bad and good.

The small, dark woman in the old cafe
Below the Cloisters brought a silver tray

Of sweets and coffee, placing it before
The man who feared a stranger at his door;

And he who ate and drank that afternoon
Had no idea that he was served by one

Who day by day rebuilt her life, yet might
Still wake herself with her own screams at night.

6/
The German Jews and the Dominicans
Were followed here by actors and musicians

From more expensive neighborhoods, intent
On finding a *lge apt, rv vu, low rent*.

We followed them, their violins and basses
And sundry other instruments in cases

Up the escalator at One Eighty-first
And out onto the street where they dispersed,

Drawn by the life that goes on after work;
Or walked with them across Fort Bennett Park

Until, whether in couples or alone,
They sought a privacy much like our own,

Sustainable for those who do not mind
The paradox that freedom lies behind

A triple-locked door in an uncertain hall.
(It *is* called an *apart*ment, after all.)

7/

Here is the river flowing as it will,
Here and beyond us always, never still,

Sustaining and sustainable for now.
---No need for us to work things out or through

When it has done that for us, as it seems,
And offers its assurances in dreams.

Tonight, it's somehow risen to our floor
And slides between the threshold and the door---

Is it rehearsing for some future case?
A window opens on another space

That we, only by leaning out into,
Can draw within: a partial river view

And a corner of the bridge, brilliantly lit
By nighttime traffic passing over it---

An image held, as we return to sleep
Of knees and elbows crouching for the leap.

Foreboding

(After Alfred Kubin, *Die Ahnung*, 1906)

What dark form has awoken
over the sleeping village
in the early morning chill?
It will have no rest until
below lie only broken
bodies among the pillage.

After 9/11

We lived in an apartment on the ridge
Running along Manhattan's northwest side,
On a street between the Cloisters and the Bridge,

On a hill George Washington once fortified
To keep his fledglings from the juggernaut
Cumbrously rolling toward them. Many died

When those defenses failed, and where they fought
Are now a ball field and a set of swings
In an urban park: old men lost in thought

Advance their pawns against opponents' kings
Or gossip beneath a sycamore's branches
All afternoon until the sunset brings

The teenagers to occupy their benches.
The park makes little of its history,
With only traces of the walls or trenches

Disputed, died by, and surrendered; we
Tread on the outline of a parapet
Pressed into the asphalt unassertively,

And on a wall descending to the street,
Observe a seriously faded plaque
Acknowledging a still-unsettled debt.

What strength of memory can summon back
That ghostly army of fifteen year olds
And their grandfathers? The Hessians attack

And the American commander folds;
We could have watched those losers made to file
Past jeering victors to the waiting holds

Of prison ships from our Tudor-style
Apartment building's roof.
                                When, without warning,
Twin towers that rose up a quarter mile

Into a cloudless sky were, early one morning,
Wreathed in the smoke from interrupted flight,
When they and what burst into them were burning

Together, like a secret brought to light,
Like something we'd imagined but not known,
The intersection of such speed, such height---

We went up on our roof and saw first one
And then the other silently unmake
Its outline, horrified, as it slid down,

Leaving a smear of ashes in its wake.
That scene, retold from other points of view,
Would grow familiar, deadening the ache:

How often we saw each jet fly into
Its target, with the same street-level gasp
Of shock and disbelief remaining new.

Little by little we would come to grasp
What *had* occurred, our incredulity
Finely abraded by the videotape's

Grim repetitions. A nonce community
Began almost at once to improvise
New rituals for curbside healing; we

Saw flowers, candles, shrines materialize
In shuttered storefronts for the benefit
Of those who'd stopped the digging with their cries

And those who hadn't. None came out of it,
None would be found still living there, beneath
The rubble scooped up out of Babel's pit:

From the clueless anonymity of death
Came fragments identified by DNA
Samples taken from bits of bone and teeth,

But that was later. In those early days
When we went outside, we walked among the few
Grieving for someone they would grieve for always,

And walked among the many others who,
Like ourselves, had no loss as profound,
But knew someone who knew someone who knew

One of the men who fell back as he wound
A spiral up the narrow, lethal staircase
Or one of those who tumbled to the ground,

The fall that our imaginations trace
Even today: the ones we most resembled,
Whose images we still cannot erase....

One night we joined our neighbors who'd assembled
For a candlelight procession: in the wind,
Each flame, protected by a cupped hand, trembled

As though to mimic an uncertain mind
Feeling its way to some insufficient word---
What certitude could our searching find?

Those who had come here to be reassured
Would leave with nothing: nothing could be said
To answer, or *have* answered, the unheard

Cries of the lost. Yet here we had been led
To gather at the entrance to the park
In a mass defined by candles for the dead,

As though they were beyond us in the dark
With those who, after *their* war had been lost,
Surrendered and were marched off to embark

On the waiting prison ships. Here now at last,
They were restored to us in a sublime
Alignment of the present with the past.

But none appeared to mock this paradigm:
All that has come before us lies below
In layer pressing upon layer....
                              Time

Is an old man telling us how, long ago,
As a child in Brooklyn he went out to play,
And prodding the summer earth with his bare toe

Discovered a bone unburied in the clay,
A remnant of those bodies that once filled
The hulks that settled into Wallabout Bay;

Time is the monument that he saw built
To turn their deaths into a victory,
Its base filled with their bones dredged out of silt;

Time is the silt grain polished by the sea,
The passageway that leads from one to naught;
Time is what argues with us constantly

Against the need to hold them all in thought,
Time is what places them beyond recall,
Against the need of the falling to be caught,

Against the woman who's begun to fall,
Against the woman who is watching from below;
Time is the photo peeling from the wall,

The busboy, who came here from Mexico
And stepped off from a window ledge, aflame;
Time is the only outcome we will know,

Against the need of those lost to be claimed
(Their last words caught in our mobile phones)
Against the need of the nameless to be named

In our city built on unacknowledged bones.

After Wang Wei

in mem. V.L.B.

On empty hills, no one to be seen,
though one can hear some distant voices---
the sun shines through branches once again
and lights upon the blue green mosses.

Poison

A few drops in a hollow ring,
Or even less on a hatpin,
Gave peace to Emperor or King
    When the Guard had fled,
And torch-lit foes were gathering
    Around his bed;

This was *the* cure for life's disease:
Observe how mindful Socrates
Drinks down the hemlock to the lees;
    Watch Charmian clasp
Her ardent mistress by the knees
    As she takes the asp.

For others, an unsought egress:
Many an ogre and ogress,
Whose motto was "Only aggress!"
    Were shown the door
(Some regarding this as Progress)
    By hellebore.

Nero, unhappy in his station,
Found poison won him swift promotion:
See Claudius, eschewing caution,
    Greedily entreat a
Servant for yet another portion
    Of the Amanita.

Secure inside his thickset walls
The tyrant ages and appalls;
Does no one hear his panicked calls
    Throughout the palace?
Another king whose kingdom falls
    To digitalis.

The rise of the middle class occurred
When all those kings had disappeared,
And tightlipped spouses, vexed or bored,
    Learned of the kick
That oatmeal has, on being stirred
    With arsenic.

And still to be found, till recently,
In the clandestine armory
Of CIA and KGB,
    Was cyanide,
Used to dispatch an enemy
    Or for suicide:

No agent's training was complete
Before he'd learned how to secrete
Upon himself the bittersweet
    End of his mission;
The little pill that, swallowed neat,
    Ensured discretion.

How innocent such poisons now
Appear to us, for even though
Fatal, they were (no matter how

Grimly horrific)
Local anesthetics, thorough-
   ly site specific:

A dose intended for the Master
Might have dispatched his dog or taster,
But our poisons yield disaster
   Without distinction,
And on a scale so much vaster,
   That our extinction

Appears to be quite plausible:
A momentary lapse, a spill,
And the stain spreads, insensible
   To our lot;
Or just consider, if you will,
   The microdot

Of some designer pathogen,
Dripped from the tip of a counterfeit pen
Or someone's nose: less 'if' than 'when,'
   When you think about it,
An end that unlike hell or heaven,
   Cannot be doubted,

And which replaces God and Devil,
Those outworn fictions, with a novel
Point of departure and arrival
   For humankind;
One with no need for the survival
   Of projective Mind

To speculate on what space is,
Or what we are. Us it erases
Without disturbing Gaia's stasis
   Or all we have wrought,
The slowly evanescing traces
   Of one dark thought.

I have no wisdom to dispel
The unbroken gloom I foretell,
Nor any wish to toll the knell
   Of parting day.
(I pinched that last bit---could you tell?
   From Thomas Gray.)

Nor would I wish the world to be
Left to the darkness or to me.
But how successful, then, could we
   Possibly *be* at
The task of reversing entropy
   By decree or fiat?

Might there not be some good reason
To cut short the losing season,
And, if not with a dose of poison,
   Find life's antidote
In blade, revolver or the noose en-
   circling one's throat?

Though we may not know where to send
The thank-you notes that we have penned
To the Imaginary Friend,

Much needs our praise,
And many need the help we tend
      To get through their days.

So if there is no God to thank,
And if the cosmic data bank
Will soon, like the stock market, tank,
      If things get dire,
Uncork one corking *Sauvignon Blanc*
      Build up the fire,

Inquire not, nor seek to know
(As Horace told us long ago)
What hour of what day you'll go;
      Just *carpe diem*,
Catch and release the ceaseless flow
      Of A.M. and P.M.

For, as John Maynard Keynes once said,
In the long run, we are all dead.
Until that happens, eat your bread
      And drink your wine
And lie with your love close in bed,
      As I with mine.

Acknowledgments

I am grateful to the editors of the following journals, in which many of the poems in this collection originally appeared, sometimes in different form or with different titles:

Alabama Literary Review	"On a Roman Perfume Bottle"
	"The Sacred Monsters"
Dark Horse	"Mind in the Trees"
The Formalist	"Poem for the Millennium"
The Hopkins Review	"Near Jeffrey's Hook"
	"Souvenir"
	"Support"
The Hudson Review	"After 9/11"
	"The Coffee House Philosopher"
	"East Side, West Side"
	"The Spaniard"
Iambs & Trochees	"Who Knows What's Best?"
Journal of Italian Translation	"The Good Soldiers"
Literary Imagination	"Ovid to His Book"
Measure	"Theory Victorious"
The New Criterion	"Some Kind of Happiness"
Pequod	"To Himself"
Rattapallax	"Autopsychography"
Smartish Pace	"Brooklyn in the Seventies"
	"For the End of the Age of Irony"
The Southwest Review	"Poison"
	"Words to Utter at Nightfall"
Stone Canoe	"The Flower Thief"
The Yale Review	"Getting Carded"

"After 9/11" was reprinted in the anthology *Best American Spiritual Writing*, 2006.

About the Author

Charles Martin's most recent book of poems, *Starting from Sleep: New and Selected Poems*, was a finalist for the Lenore Marshall Award of the Academy of American Poets in 2003. His verse translation of the *Metamorphoses* of Ovid received the Harold Morton Landon Award from the Academy of American Poets in 2004. In 2005, he received an Award for Literature from the American Academy of Arts and Letters. His other books of poems include *Steal the Bacon* and *What the Darkness Proposes*, and a translation, *The Poems of Catullus*, all published by the Johns Hopkins University Press. Other work includes *Catullus*, a critical introduction to the Latin poet. He is the recipient of a Bess Hokin Prize from *Poetry*, a Pushcart Prize, and fellowships from the Ingram Merrill Foundation and the National Endowment for the Arts. He served as Poet in Residence at the Cathedral of St. John the Divine in New York from 2005 to 2009.